SWITZERLAND 2016 HUMAN RIGHTS REPORT

EXECUTIVE SUMMARY

The Swiss Confederation is a constitutional republic with a federal structure. Legislative authority resides in a bicameral parliament (Federal Assembly) consisting of the 46-member Council of States and the 200-member National Council. Federal elections were held in October 2015 and were generally considered free and fair. Parliament elects the executive leadership (the seven-member Federal Council) every four years, and did so in December 2015. A four-party coalition made up the Federal Council.

Civilian authorities maintained effective control over the security forces.

The most significant problems included the occasional use of excessive force by security forces, particularly in connection with the interrogation of drug suspects in the canton of Geneva, arrests and deportations of asylum seekers, and in detention facilities. Authorities reportedly treated pretrial detainees worse than convicted criminals and sometimes subjected asylum seekers to lengthy detention and mistreatment. Societal discrimination against Roma, members of other minorities, and immigrants also occurred.

Other human rights problems included overcrowded prisons, isolation of prisoners up to 23 hours a day, inadequate health facilities in some prisons, occasional mixing of detainees and convicts, instances of denial of access to a lawyer and notification of family upon arrest, mixing of men and women in asylum detention centers, shortages of adequate housing for migrants and asylum seekers, some corruption in government, violence against women, forced marriages and female genital mutilation/cutting among some immigrant groups, child abuse, anti-Semitic incidents, trafficking in persons, employers' interference with trade union rights, some instances of forced labor, and discrimination in pay and employment for women and older workers.

The government took steps to prosecute and punish officials who committed violations, whether in the security services or elsewhere in the government.

Section 1. Respect for the Integrity of the Person, Including Freedom from:

a. Arbitrary Deprivation of Life and other Unlawful or Politically Motivated Killings

There were no reports that the government or its agents committed arbitrary or unlawful killings.

b. Disappearance

There were no reports of politically motivated disappearances.

c. Torture and Other Cruel, Inhuman, or Degrading Treatment or Punishment

The constitution prohibits such practices. There were isolated reports that individual police officers used excessive force and engaged in degrading treatment while making arrests.

In June Bern's high court rejected the appeal of two police officers who were sentenced by the canton's regional court in October 2015 to separate suspended fines for kicking an unruly man at a train station's police post, dragging him through a pool of his own urine, and throwing his jacket into the pool.

In April the district court of Bremgarten in the canton of Aargau sentenced a police officer to a suspended fine for abuse of authority, damage to property, and trespassing in a domestic violence incident in 2009 in which the officer stormed the apartment of a violent Serbian-origin man who had threatened his own family. The court deemed the officer's use of force to gain access to the property excessive. The court sentenced a second police officer involved in the incident to a suspended fine for committing grievous bodily harm in self-defense after shooting the man twice.

On June 23, the Council of Europe's Committee for the Prevention of Torture (CPT), in its report on its visit to the country in 2015, observed "a phenomenon of police violence seemed to persist" in the canton of Geneva. It collected "numerous allegations of mistreatment" during interrogation by members of the Drug Task Force, who struck detainees with fists and bludgeons, sometimes while they were blindfolded. In the prison at Geneva's Champ-Dollon, the CPT heard allegations of excessive use of force and deliberate violence by the guards.

In 2015 the National Commission for the Prevention of Torture (NCPT), an independent governmental organization, condemned Bern's Thorberg Prison for chaining unruly detainees against a wall for several hours. It further found that most juvenile detention centers did not adequately document the use of restraining measures against prisoners.

Prison and Detention Center Conditions

Notwithstanding some inadequate facilities, prison and detention center conditions usually met international standards.

Physical Conditions: Prison overcrowding remained a problem, especially in the French-speaking part of the country. During the year Geneva's Champ-Dollon Prison continued to be the most crowded facility, with a population of more than 170 percent of design capacity. As of April more than 670 inmates occupied the prison's 390 available spaces, with single cells often occupied by up to three persons. The CPT found the cells in Geneva's police station and Geneva's Paquis police station so small that they should be used only for short times. The canton of Vaud's La Croisee Prison had an occupancy rate of 152 percent.

In August the federal court dismissed the complaints of five Champ-Dollon Prison inmates for a reduction of their sentences and financial compensation of up to 66,000 Swiss francs ($64,224) for allegedly having been held in pretrial detention for as many as 220 days. The prisoners also complained about the small size of their cells and a lack of access to outdoor spaces. The federal court ruled the complainants had not acted in good faith, as they reportedly only raised the issue of mistreatment after receiving their sentences. Later in the same month, however, the federal court approved a separate complaint of another Champ-Dollon prisoner who was allegedly held in a cell of 43 square feet for 599 days.

The NCPT found that youths in pretrial detention were often restricted in their movement and given limited access to external contacts, with some spending up to 20 hours in their cells. The nongovernmental organization (NGO) Terre des Hommes criticized the government's placing of underage asylum seekers in administrative detention, arguing the conditions of incarceration undermined the UN Convention on the Rights of the Child.

As of October press sources reported at least four suicides during the year. According to the Federal Office for Statistics, in 2014, the last year for which data were available, there were 15 deaths in confinement, including nine suicides.

The CPT noted inadequate health care in the prisons at La Farera, La Stampa, and in Schwyz. It also recommended that 14 days be made the maximum period of solitary confinement throughout the country.

In July the NCPT's sixth annual report focused on pretrial conditions and preventive detention centers, citing inadequate separation of different types of prisoners, excessive incarceration periods of as many as 23 hours a day, lack of occupational activities and physical exercise opportunities, and restrictive access to external contacts, including total telephone bans, and limiting visitors to once a week for half an hour. The NCPT found that pretrial detainees were treated worse than convicted criminals, with some cantons keeping pretrial prisoners in their cells for up to 23 hours a day. The commission noted incidents of prison overcrowding, lengthy pretrial detention and solitary confinement, and a shortage of prison guards. The commission also reported that foreigners awaiting deportation occasionally had little space for physical exercise and free movement.

In 2015 the NCPT visited nine prisons in 11 cantons, including inspections of juvenile detention facilities in numerous cantons. While the commission deemed overall conditions at the institutions to be adequate, it found some prisons to be underresourced and overcrowded. The committee criticized the Pfaeffikon Prison in Zurich for banning persons in pretrial detention from using the phone and for limiting prisoners' ability to communicate with their lawyers.

Administration: There was no ombudsman or comparable authority available at the national level to respond to complaints, but a number of cantons maintained cantonal ombudsmen and mediation boards that acted on behalf of prisoners and detainees to address complaints related to their detention. Such resources were more readily available in the larger, more populous cantons than in smaller, less populated ones. The youth detention facility in the canton of Fribourg failed to keep records of disciplinary actions against inmates.

Independent Monitoring: The government permitted independent monitoring of conditions in prisons and asylum reception centers by local and international human rights groups, the media, and the International Committee of the Red Cross. The CPT carried out its latest periodic visit to the country in April 2015. Local groups enjoyed a high degree of independence.

Improvements: The prison in Sion increased its number of occupational activities. The prison in Fribourg expanded its outdoor recreational areas, discontinued admitting youths and confining women in pretrial detention, and only in rare and exceptional cases kept foreigners in administrative detention.

d. Arbitrary Arrest or Detention

The constitution prohibits arbitrary arrest and detention, and the government generally observed these prohibitions.

Role of the Police and Security Apparatus

The federal police maintain internal security. The army is responsible for external security but also has some domestic security responsibilities. The police report to the Federal Department of Justice and Police, while the army reports to the Federal Department of Defense, Civil Protection, and Sport. The State Secretariat for Migration (SEM) reports to the Federal Department of Justice and Police and is responsible for granting immigrant visas and residence/work permits, evaluating asylum and refugee applications, and managing deportations. The Swiss Border Guard reports to the Federal Department of Finance and is responsible for registering asylum seekers, and fighting illegal migration and transborder crime.

Civilian authorities maintained effective control over the police and the army, and the government has effective mechanisms to investigate and punish abuse and corruption. Cantonal state prosecutors and police generally investigated security force violence; in some cantons; however, the ombudsman's office investigated such cases. In addition to its coordination and analytical responsibilities, the Federal Office of Police may pursue its own investigations under the supervision of the attorney general in cases of organized crime, money laundering, and corruption.

Arrest Procedures and Treatment of Detainees

By law police must apprehend criminal suspects based on warrants issued by a duly authorized official unless responding to a specific and immediate danger. In most instances authorities may not hold a suspect more than 24 hours before bringing him or her before a prosecutor or investigating magistrate, who must either formally charge a detainee or order his or her release. Immigration authorities may detain asylum seekers and other foreigners without valid documents up to 96 hours without an arrest warrant. There is a functioning bail system, and courts granted release on personal recognizance or bail unless the magistrate believed the person charged to be dangerous or a flight risk.

Alternatives to bail include having suspects report to probation officers and imposing restraining orders on suspects. Authorities may deny a suspect legal counsel at the time of detention or initial questioning, but the suspect has the right to choose and contact an attorney before being charged. The state provides free legal assistance for indigents charged with crimes with a possible prison sentence. According to the CPT, detainees often did not have access to a lawyer for several hours after arrest. Authorities may restrict family members' access to prevent evidence tampering, but authorities require law enforcement officials to inform close relatives promptly of the detention. The CPT reported that the right to inform the families of arrests "was not always recognized" and that "it was not uncommon" for the delay to last several hours. It condemned the denial of contacts, including visits and telephone calls, to prisoners awaiting judgment for up to several months.

The law allows police to detain young offenders for a "minimal period" but does not explicitly state the length. In actuality, without an arraignment or arrest warrant, police may detain young offenders for a maximum of 24 hours (48 hours during weekends). The CPT recommended that authorities never interrogate a minor or force a minor to make a statement in the absence of a lawyer.

Arbitrary Arrest: There were occasional reports of arbitrary arrest. In July the federal court overturned a 2015 ruling by Zurich's high court that suspended proceedings against three police officers accused of beating, kicking, and temporarily chaining up a gay man at a police station in 2011 after the man complained about not being able to bring harassment charges against two youths. The police officers allegedly also prevented the man from contacting his partner about bringing him his HIV medication while in custody. The federal court resubmitted the case to Zurich's public prosecutor, where it has been pending since September.

Pretrial Detention: The NGO Humanrights.ch and local media reported that lengthy pretrial detention was a problem. In 2015 approximately 27 percent of all prisoners were in pretrial detention. The country's highest court ruled pretrial detention must not exceed the length of the expected sentence for the crime for which a suspect is charged. Humanrights.ch noted that authorities often used pretrial detention to pressure suspects into admissions of guilt.

Detainee's Ability to Challenge Lawfulness of Detention before a Court: Arrested or detained persons are entitled to challenge in court the legal or arbitrary nature of their detention and to obtain prompt release. Unlawfully detained persons and persons found innocent may appeal to the courts for compensation.

Protracted Detention of Rejected Asylum Seekers or Stateless Persons: The NGO Terre des Hommes criticized the government's placement of underage asylum seekers in administrative detention, arguing the incarceration conditions undermined the UN Convention on the Rights of the Child. According to the NCPT's 2013 and 2014 reports, measures against asylum seekers awaiting deportation were often harsher than against individuals in pretrial detention. In a 2014 report, the NGO Terre des Femmes noted female asylum seekers housed in overcrowded coed facilities risked becoming victims of sexual harassment and violence, due to the nonseparation of men and women. The report further cited a lack of recreational rooms, work opportunities, and social activities.

e. Denial of Fair Public Trial

The constitution provides for an independent judiciary, and the government generally respected judicial independence.

Trial Procedures

The constitution provides for the right to a fair public trial, and an independent judiciary generally enforced this right.

Defendants enjoy a presumption of innocence. Defendants have the right to be informed promptly and in detail of the charges with free interpretation as necessary from the moment charged through all appeals. Trials are public and held without undue delay. Defendants are entitled to be present at their trial. They have the right to consult with an attorney in a timely manner, and the courts may provide an attorney at public expense if a defendant faces serious criminal charges. Defendants have adequate time and facilities to prepare a defense. They have the right to access government-held evidence, to confront and question witnesses, and to present witnesses and evidence. Defendants may not be compelled to testify or confess guilt. They have the right to appeal, ultimately to the Federal Tribunal, the country's highest court. Sentences for youths up to age 15 may be for no longer than one year. For youth offenders 16 or older, sentences may be up to four years. Authorities generally respected these rights and extended them to all citizens.

Military courts may try civilians charged with revealing military secrets, such as classified military documents or classified military locations and installations. There were no reports that military courts tried any civilians during the year.

Political Prisoners and Detainees

There were no reports of political prisoners or detainees.

Civil Judicial Procedures and Remedies

There is an independent and impartial judiciary in civil matters. Citizens have access to a court to bring lawsuits seeking damages for or cessation of a human rights violation. Individuals and organizations may appeal adverse domestic decisions to regional human rights bodies, such as the European Court of Human Rights.

f. Arbitrary or Unlawful Interference with Privacy, Family, Home, or Correspondence

The constitution prohibits such actions, and there were no reports the government failed to respect these prohibitions.

Section 2. Respect for Civil Liberties, Including:

a. Freedom of Speech and Press

The constitution provides for freedom of speech and press, although the law restricts speech involving racial hatred and denial of crimes against humanity. The government generally respected these rights. An independent press, an effective judiciary, and a functioning democratic political system combined to promote freedom of speech and press.

Freedom of Speech and Expression: The law prohibits hate speech, such as public incitement to racial hatred or discrimination, spreading racist ideology, and denying crimes against humanity, including via electronic means. It provides for punishment of violators by monetary fines and imprisonment of up to three years. There were several convictions under this law during the year (see section 6, Anti-Semitism and National/Racial/Ethnic Minorities).

<u>Press and Media Freedoms</u>: Independent media were active and expressed a wide variety of views. The law's restrictions on hate speech and denial of crimes against humanity apply to print, broadcast, and online newspapers/journals. According to federal law, it is a crime to publish information based on leaked "secret official discussions."

Internet Freedom

The government did not restrict or disrupt access to the internet or censor online content, and there were no credible reports the government monitored private online communications without appropriate legal authority. According to the Federal Office of Statistics, 89 percent of the population over 14 years of age used the internet during the year.

Academic Freedom and Cultural Events

There were no government restrictions on academic freedom or cultural events.

b. Freedom of Peaceful Assembly and Association

The constitution provides for the freedoms of assembly and association, and the government generally respected these rights.

c. Freedom of Religion

See the Department of State's *International Religious Freedom Report* at www.state.gov/religiousfreedomreport/.

d. Freedom of Movement, Internally Displaced Persons, Protection of Refugees, and Stateless Persons

The constitution provides for freedom of internal movement, foreign travel, emigration, and repatriation, and the government generally respected these rights.

<u>Abuse of Migrants, Refugees, and Stateless Persons</u>: Authorities may detain asylum seekers who inhibit authorities' processing of their asylum requests, subject to judicial review, for up to six months while adjudicating their applications. The government may detain rejected applicants for up to three months to ensure they do not go into hiding prior to forced deportation, or up to 18 months if repatriation posed special obstacles. The government may detain minors between the ages of

15 and 18 for up to 12 months pending repatriation. Authorities generally instructed refused asylum seekers to leave voluntarily but could forcibly repatriate those who refused.

NGO Swiss Refugee Aid condemned the cantons for not providing adequate care and support for unaccompanied minor asylum seekers. On August 29, Amnesty International accused the government of preventing numerous unaccompanied minor migrants from crossing the country's southern border from Italy, although they allegedly sought asylum and protection. The report also criticized the government for disregarding international agreements by refusing irregular or undocumented migrants preliminary asylum proceedings and preventing the reunification of separated families.

On July 5, the NCPT released its annual report on deportation flights. Between April 2015 and April 2016, the country forcibly deported 328 persons, including 18 families and 36 children, to their countries of origin on 53 repatriation flights. NCPT observers criticized isolated instances of Tasers used against deportees and the separation of family members prior to deportation. While there was less frequent use of restraining measures to immobilize asylum seekers who threatened resistance, the NCPT documented one case of an unruly parent being placed in body shackles in front of his children. The NCPT also condemned officials in the cantons of Geneva, Neuchatel, Vaud, and Valais for wearing balaclava-like masks when summoning individuals for deportation.

Local media reported a significant increase in conflicts among asylum seekers in federal asylum centers between January and April, with security personnel intervening 240 times to de-escalate clashes. Reports of interventions in 2015 ranged from 111 to 122. Swiss Refugee Aid attributed the rise in conflicts to the heightened psychological pressure on asylum seekers as a result of authorities taking longer than in 2015 to relocate asylum seekers from federal centers to cantonal asylum homes. Swiss Refugee Aid called on the government to invest more in support measures for asylum seekers.

In August a fire at an asylum center in Bern led to the evacuation of numerous asylum seekers. A separate fire during the same month completely burned down an asylum center housing 10 people in Solothurn's Biberist municipality. Authorities moved the asylum seekers to the municipality's military barracks.

In 2014 a Syrian asylum seeker suffered a stillbirth while being deported to Italy due to the alleged refusal of officials to provide medical assistance. A postmortem report confirmed the child died 12 hours before the stillbirth, which according to media reports, supported claims of misconduct and neglect by border guard officers. Authorities turned the case over to a military tribunal, where it was pending as of year's end.

Between January and July, the Federal Coordination Unit against Forced Marriages received 119 notifications of forced marriages involving minors, 26 of which involved girls under the age of 16 years. Victims came mainly from Iraqi, Syrian, Eritrean, Afghani, and Somali communities. In 2015 media reports estimated that NGOs and authorities usually identified 250 victims each year, both adults and minors. Local media attributed the significant rise in forced marriages of minors to the continued migrant influx, while the Coordination Unit credited more effective awareness raising with the increase in victim identification. While one NGO working with victims of forced marriage continued to assist on average five victims each week, it documented a marked increase in underage victims.

NGOs working with refugees continued to complain that officials often effectively denied detained asylum seekers proper legal representation in deportation cases due to their financial inability to hire an attorney. Authorities provided free legal assistance only during the initial phase of the asylum application and in cases of serious criminal offenses, deeming deportation of asylum seekers an administrative, rather than a judicial, process.

The government cooperated with the Office of the UN High Commissioner for Refugees (UNHCR) and other humanitarian organizations in providing protection and assistance to refugees, asylum seekers, stateless persons, and other persons of concern.

Protection of Refugees

<u>Access to Asylum</u>: The law provides for the granting of asylum or refugee status, and the government established a system for providing protection to refugees. The government required asylum applicants to provide documentation verifying their identity within 48 hours of completing their applications; authorities refused to process applications of asylum seekers unable to provide a credible justification for their lack of acceptable documents or to show evidence of persecution.

In June voters approved the revision of the country's asylum law to expedite the asylum process by reducing processing times to a maximum of 140 days, as well as to increase financial aid and to provide free legal help to asylum seekers. The country's embassies abroad do not accept asylum requests, and conscientious objectors and army deserters do not automatically qualify for refugee status.

Safe Country of Origin/Transit: The SEM relied on a list of "safe countries." Asylum seekers who originated from or transited these countries generally were ineligible for asylum. The country is a signatory to the EU's Dublin III Regulation.

Refoulement: The constitution prohibits the deportation of refugees who face persecution in their countries of origin and also states that no one may be sent to a country where they might face torture or other degrading and cruel acts. While the government generally did not force asylum seekers to return to countries where their lives or freedom may be threatened, there were reportedly exceptions. In July the SEM announced it would allow deportations to all parts of Sri Lanka, contingent on case-by-case evaluations. Swiss Refugee Aid criticized the new practice, calling the revisions premature in light of the organization's assessment that northern Sri Lanka was still unsafe for government dissidents.

Employment: The law prohibits asylum seekers from working during the first three months following their arrival in the country, and authorities can extend that prohibition for an additional three months if the SEM rejects the asylum application within the first three months. After three months asylum seekers may seek employment in industries with labor shortages, such as in the hospitality, construction, health-care, or agricultural sectors.

Access to Basic Services: The cantons assumed the main responsibility for providing housing, general assistance, and care to asylum applicants during the processing phase. Shortages of sufficient and appropriate housing for asylum seekers remained a problem. Asylum seekers have the right to access basic medical care, and the children of asylum seekers are entitled to attend school until ninth grade (the last year for which school is mandatory). NGOs and volunteers generally conducted language classes for asylum seekers.

To accommodate increasing numbers of asylum seekers, the SEM continued to house hundreds of asylum seekers in remote rural areas or in decommissioned military establishments--several of them underground--that were retrofitted to serve as short-term housing.

Durable Solutions: In December the government announced it would accept an additional 2,000 Syrian refugees over the next two years as part of a UNHCR resettlement program. In March 2015 the government had agreed to accept 3,000 Syrian refugees between 2015 and 2018 under the UNHCR resettlement program. Of these, 357 had arrived in the country as of March.

Temporary Protection: In 2015 the government granted temporary admission to 7,787 individuals, 2,534 of whom the government designated as refugees.

In 2015 Amnesty International and UNHCR criticized the country for granting refugee status to only 40 percent of Syrian asylum seekers. Other Syrian asylum seekers were admitted as "temporarily admitted refugees." Those awarded temporary refugee status faced more restrictions on family reunification.

Section 3. Freedom to Participate in the Political Process

The constitution provides citizens the ability to choose their government in free and fair periodic elections held by secret ballot and based on universal and equal suffrage.

Elections and Political Participation

Recent Elections: In October 2015 voters elected parliamentary representatives for the National Council and the Council of States. Runoff elections for the Council of States in 12 of the 26 cantons were completed in November 2015. Parliament elected the executive leadership (the seven-member Federal Council) in December 2015. Observers considered the elections free and fair.

Participation of Women and Minorities: No laws limit the participation of women and members of minorities in the political process, and women and minorities participated. A UN report on gender equality published in November, however, found that "structural barriers and gender bias" led to fewer female parliamentarians in both houses.

Section 4. Corruption and Lack of Transparency in Government

The law provides criminal penalties for corruption by officials, and the government generally implemented the law effectively. There were isolated reports of government corruption during the year.

Corruption: Investigating and prosecuting government corruption is a federal responsibility. In its third interim report, published on August 25, the Group of

States against Corruption (GRECO) evaluated the government's progress on fighting corruption as "overall unsatisfactory." The report again criticized the government's continued lack of statutory regulations on political party financing. GRECO, however, commended parliament's passage of legislation in September 2015 that made bribery in the private sector a criminal offense. Federal police and public prosecutors also adopted an anonymous whistleblower hotline for members of the public to report suspicious activities to state authorities.

Transparency International Switzerland called on the country to improve its fight against international corruption cases, to protect whistle-blowers better, and to pass legislation on the transparency of party and election campaign funding.

In November the federal criminal court sentenced the former information technology head of the Federal Office for the Environment to a prison sentence of two and a half years, of which 15 months were suspended, and an additional suspended fine for committing passive bribery and misconduct in public office. The man allegedly accepted money and gifts between 2007 and 2010 in exchange for granting business contracts to select information technology companies recommended by a private-sector colleague.

Financial Disclosure: Members of the Federal Assembly must disclose annually their financial interests, professional activities, supervisory board or executive body memberships, and activities as consultants or paid experts. A majority of cantons required members of cantonal parliaments to disclose their financial interests.

Public Access to Information: The constitution requires the government to inform the public about its activities, and government information was available to all persons living in the country, including foreign media. The law provides for public access to government documents. Authorities enforced the law, and access to public information was readily available. After the Swiss Press Council criticized the courts for only publishing judgments once a ruling has taken effect, in June the Federal Court ruled that court judgments must be published and made publicly available as soon as a ruling has been made.

Section 5. Governmental Attitude Regarding International and Nongovernmental Investigation of Alleged Violations of Human Rights

A variety of domestic and international human rights groups generally operated without government restriction, investigating and publishing their findings on human rights cases. Government officials were cooperative and responsive to their views.

Government Human Rights Bodies: The Swiss Center for Human Rights (SCHR), created by the Federal Department of Foreign Affairs and the Federal Department of Justice and Police, consists of a network of universities and human rights experts responsible for strengthening and supporting human rights capacities and bridging gaps between federal and cantonal authorities on human rights problems. The SCHR hosted presentations and published reports on human rights themes, such as on the deprivation of liberty, access to justice, and the rights of vulnerable groups in society.

There were 14 cantonal ombudsman offices that also assessed cases of police misconduct.

Section 6. Discrimination, Societal Abuses, and Trafficking in Persons

Women

Rape and Domestic Violence: Rape, including spousal rape, is a statutory offense. Penalties for rape range from one to 10 years in prison. The government effectively prosecuted individuals accused of such crimes.

NGOs such as Terre des Femmes, Vivre Sans Violence, and the umbrella organization for women's shelters noted that violence against women remained a serious problem. Domestic violence resulted in the deaths of 36 individuals in 2015. In 2015 police registered 17,297 cases linked to domestic violence or domestic abuse. The law penalizes domestic violence and stalking. A court may order an abusive spouse to leave the family home temporarily.

Specialized government agencies, numerous NGOs, and nearly a dozen private or government-sponsored hotlines provided help, counseling, and legal assistance to victims of domestic violence. Official women's shelters had average occupancy rates between 70 and 90 percent, and many shelters reached 100 percent capacity, particularly in the northwest of the country. Demand for shelter space regularly exceeded capacity, with some victims turned away and housed in alternative accommodations, such as in hotels or specialized institutions. A special unit in the Office for Gender Equality of the Federal Department of Home Affairs focused on domestic violence. Most cantonal police forces included specially trained domestic violence units. A majority of cantons had administrative units to coordinate the activities of law enforcement agencies, prosecutors, and victims assistance groups.

A 2014 report on local women's shelters published by the conference of cantonal social directors concluded that most victims were foreign women from low-income families and that a three-fold increase in shelter spaces was needed nationally to assist all survivors adequately. The report further cited a lack of financial resources and a discrepancy in services offered across the cantons.

On November 25, the NGO Christian Peace Service organized a government-supported campaign on the influence of gender stereotypes on violence against women that included approximately 50 participating organizations and 70 public awareness events across the country.

Female Genital Mutilation/Cutting (FGM/C): FGM/C is illegal and punishable by up to 10 years' imprisonment. For the period 2016-19, the Federal Office for Health and the SEM committed to support an information, counseling, and prevention network against FGM/C run by the NGOs Caritas, Terres des Femmes, Sexual Health Switzerland, and the SCHR. The NGO Caritas, however, criticized the continued absence of a national strategy against FGM/C and a lack of cantonal programs on the issue.

No cases of FGM/C were brought to court in 2015. According to government and NGO estimates, approximately 15,000 women and girls, primarily from Somalia, Eritrea, Ethiopia, Sudan, and Egypt, were affected by, or at risk of, FGM/C.

In 2014 the women's human rights organization Terre des Femmes, in conjunction with the Federal Office of Public Health, published an assessment of FGM/C in the country. Several federal offices, in collaboration with NGOs and academic institutions, implemented educational and preventative measures aimed at vulnerable communities and relevant authorities, including a mediation service. The cantons of Geneva, Neuchatel, Vaud, and Fribourg carried out selective awareness-raising activities and measures, while other cantons began similar awareness-raising efforts.

Sexual Harassment: The law prohibits sexual harassment and facilitates legal remedies for those claiming discrimination or harassment in the workplace. Special legal protection against the dismissal of a claimant, however, is only temporary. Employers failing to take reasonable measures to prevent sexual harassment are liable for damages up to the equivalent of six months' salary.

<u>Reproductive Rights</u>: The government recognized the right of couples and individuals to decide the number, spacing, and timing of their children; manage their reproductive health; and have access to the information and means to do so, free from discrimination, coercion, or violence.

<u>Discrimination</u>: The constitution and the law provide for the same legal status and rights for women as for men in matters of labor and employment. The constitution provides for the same legal status and rights for women as for men. The civil law provides for the same legal status and rights for women as for men in matters of property and inheritance. In 2015 parliament passed revisions to the civil law ensuring a more equitable division of pension funds during divorce retroactive to all divorces since 2000.

In November a UN report concluded that prevailing stereotypes about the roles and responsibilities of women and men in the family and in society, along with "deep-rooted patriarchal attitudes," impeded progress on gender equality. The report further stated that stereotyped media portrayals and negative images of ethnic minority women and migrant women undermined their ability to integrate into society.

A 2014 report of the Federal Office for Gender Equality and the Federal Commission on Women outlined progress in women's education levels and earning potential over the previous 15 years. Despite advances, the report concluded educated women were twice as likely to be poor than educated men, mostly because women remained the primary family caregivers and were not monetarily compensated for the time spent caring for their children or other relatives. The report highlighted that 19 percent of women (compared with 7 percent of men) were low wage earners in 2010, which, coupled with their primary caregiver responsibilities, exposed them to a high poverty risk and negative consequences in the labor market and social security system. Many cantons and some large cities had equality offices to handle gender problems.

Children

<u>Birth Registration</u>: Citizenship derives from one's parents; a single parent may convey citizenship. Authorities registered births immediately. There are no negative repercussions for delayed registration in cases of home delivery.

<u>Child Abuse</u>: Child abuse was a significant problem. In 2015 an expert group for child protection in children's clinics registered 1,388 cases of child abuse, of which 20 percent involved sexual abuse and 28 percent physical abuse. The group observed a noticeable increase in psychological abuse, which constituted 31 percent of reported cases. It expressed concern over the high rate of infant victims, with 18 percent of the registered children under the age of one year. As in 2014 one infant died from physical abuse. Approximately 20 percent of cases involved neglect. Doctors filed criminal charges against abusive parents in 85 instances.

<u>Early and Forced Marriage</u>: The legal minimum age of marriage is 18 years. The law prohibits forced marriage and provides for penalties of up to five years in prison, and denies permission to enter the country to visa applicants suspected of involvement in a forced marriage. Victims of forced marriage already residing in the country may remain and may change their marital status from "married" to "single" without a requirement to record a divorce. According to police statistics, 13 individuals were victims of forced marriage in 2015 (see also section 2.d.).

<u>Female Genital Mutilation/Cutting</u>: See information for girls under 18 in women's section above.

<u>Sexual Exploitation of Children</u>: The production, possession, distribution, or downloading of internet pornography that involves children is illegal and punishable by fines or a maximum sentence of one year in prison. With few exceptions, the law designates 16 as the minimum age for consensual sex. The law permits consensual sex below the age of 16 in cases where one partner is not more than three years older than the other. The maximum penalty for statutory rape is imprisonment for 10 years. The Cybercrime Coordination Unit's mandate included preventing and prosecuting crimes involving the sexual exploitation of children online.

The law prohibits prostitution of persons under the age of 18 and punishes pimps of underage prostitutes with prison sentences of up to 10 years. It provides for sentences of up to three years in prison for persons engaging in commercial sex with an underage prostitute.

<u>International Child Abductions</u>: The country is a party to the 1980 Hague Convention on the Civil Aspects of International Child Abduction. See the Department of State's *Annual Report on International Parental Child Abduction* at travel.state.gov/content/childabduction/en/legal/compliance.html.

Anti-Semitism

According to the Swiss Federation of Jewish Communities (SIG/FSCI), approximately 18,000 Jewish individuals resided in the country as of November. The largest Jewish communities were in Zurich, Geneva, Lausanne, Basel, and Bern.

In 2015 the SIG/FSCI recorded a marked decrease in anti-Semitic statements, acts, and online activity, which it attributed to the de-escalation of the Gaza conflict and greater social awareness from the widespread media coverage of the many anti-Semitic incidents and subsequent criminal investigations that occurred in 2014. The *2015 Anti-Semitism Report*, produced jointly by the SIG/FSCI and the Foundation against Racism and Anti-Semitism, cited 16 anti-Semitic incidents (excluding anti-Semitic hate speech online) in the German-speaking part of the country in 2015, a quarter of the number in 2014. The report documented two physical assaults against Jews.

In 2015 the Geneva-based Intercommunity Center for Coordination against Anti-Semitism and Defamation (CICAD) reported 164 anti-Semitic incidents in the French-speaking region, of which it deemed 11 serious. Although CICAD also recorded a decrease in anti-Semitic incidents, the report stressed that the number of documented incidents in 2015 was among the highest during its 12-year existence. The report also noted that the most anti-Semitic incidents occurred during January and February following the terror attacks in Paris and Copenhagen. According to local media reports, concerns within the Jewish community about the increased terror threat against Jews prompted the Federal Department of Defense, Civil Protection, and Sport to establish a working group to devise adequate protection measures for Jewish institutions.

In January the public prosecutor's office of the canton of Ticino initiated criminal proceedings against a police sergeant for posting pictures and quotes by Hitler and Mussolini on his Facebook page. The public prosecutor sentenced the man to a suspended monetary fine for inciting racism.

In November the SIG lodged a police complaint against a neo-Nazi group for song lyrics calling for the death of Swiss Jews. The group had also issued death threats against leading Swiss Jews, among them SIG/FSCI President Herbert Winter, and targeted politicians and other public personalities. In October neo-Nazi groups held two concerts, one of which an estimated 5,000 far-right activists attended.

As part of the national census, the Federal Council completed a five-year pilot project in 2015 to survey racist and discriminatory sentiments nationwide, including racism, anti-Muslim sentiment, anti-Semitism, xenophobia, and intolerance. Anti-Semitic attitudes remained stable throughout the test period, with one participant in 10 admitting to negative opinions about Jews in each of the biannual surveys.

Trafficking in Persons

See the Department of State's *Trafficking in Persons Report* at www.state.gov/j/tip/rls/tiprpt/.

Persons with Disabilities

The constitution and federal law prohibit discrimination against persons with physical, sensory, intellectual, and mental disabilities in employment, education, air travel and other transportation, access to health care, the judicial system, and the provision of other state services, and the government generally enforced the prohibition. The law mandates access to public buildings and government services for persons with disabilities, and the government generally enforced these provisions.

The CPT reported that some persons were hospitalized in conditions inappropriate to their mental disabilities. Those in high-security confinement were isolated with strictly minimal contacts with the staff and then through bars and occasional contacts with a psychiatrist or psychologist.

The Federal Equal Opportunity Office for Persons with Disabilities promoted awareness of the law and respect for the rights of individuals with disabilities through counseling and financial support for projects to facilitate their integration in society and the labor market.

Procap, one of the country's largest organizations for persons with disabilities, noted that pensioners with disabilities often struggled to maintain their living standards, with up to 40 percent relying on supplementary benefits. In 2015 several other NGOs criticized the canton of Zurich for being unprepared to deal with and care for an increasing number of persons with disabilities reaching retirement age.

In June the government released its first report for implementing the UN Convention on the Rights of Persons with Disabilities. The report concluded that the country's equality law for persons with disabilities, the revisions to the federal disability insurance, and the adult protection law had brought about significant improvements for persons with disabilities. Procap however maintained that persons with disabilities remained disadvantaged in terms of sufficient access to postcompulsory education, general services, and leisure activities.

In August an NGO criticized the canton of Zurich for subsidizing the living costs of persons with disabilities only if they reside in assisted living institutions. The group called on the canton to provide more alternatives to assisted living and to allow persons with disabilities to decide freely the use of their individually assigned disability support funds.

In 2015 the Bern University of Applied Sciences released a study citing the lack of a direct and nonbureaucratic national contact point for reporting abuse against persons with disabilities. The report concluded that, despite the existence of a broad and diverse range of specialist units, the availability of services for such persons was confusing and unclear.

National/Racial/Ethnic Minorities

Right-wing extremists, including skinheads, who expressed hostility toward foreigners, ethnic and religious minorities, and immigrants, continued to be active.

In July the public prosecutor's office of the canton of Valais initiated criminal proceedings against a lower house parliamentarian from the right-wing Swiss People's Party (SVP) after the man publicly condoned the killing of a Muslim in a St. Gallen mosque in 2015 with a tweet that read "We want more!" The case was pending as of October.

In March the high court of Bern affirmed the criminal court of Bern-Mittelland's 2015 sentencing of two members of the SVP for breaching the antiracism law following the publication of a poster in 2011 titled "Kosovars slice up Swiss citizens." The poster was used to collect signatures for the anti-immigration initiative and referred to a Kosovar badly injuring a Swiss citizen in a violent incident several days prior to the launch of the anti-immigration campaign. The high court however reduced the sentences to suspended fines of 45 Swiss francs ($44) per day instead of the original suspended fines of 60 Swiss francs ($58) per day.

In June the Consulting Network for Racism Victims released its report for 2015, documenting an increase in racism against black persons and incidents of Islamophobia. While the report noted that most incidents of racial discrimination were verbal and occurred primarily in the workplace, 16 incidents involved physical attacks against minorities. The extent of right-wing populism and extremism remained unchanged over the previous year. The report examined 239 incidents, 16 of which involved ethnic profiling, compiled by 18 different consulting services. During the year the Federal Commission against Racism noted a lack of antiracism education in most public schools and stressed the need to address society's growing xenophobia towards asylum seekers and refugees.

In November a UN report concluded that stereotyped media portrayals and negative images of ethnic minority women and migrant women undermined their ability to integrate into society.

Also in November the federal court declared a planned cantonal initiative by the SVP aimed at closing down the University of Fribourg's Islam Center and preventing the local education of imams as invalid. The court ruled the initiative Islamophobic and in breach of the antidiscrimination law.

In 2014 the European Commission against Racism and Intolerance (ECRI) reported that individuals continued to use xenophobic and racist political discourse to target minority groups, such as Muslims, blacks, refugees, the Yenish, and Romani groups, thereby exacerbating their negative image and poor living conditions. Racial profiling subjected the black community in particular to police controls, such as public arrests and body searches for drugs.

While the government recognized the Yenish as a minority group with approximately 35,000 residents in the country, ECRI noted a persistent lack of proper camping facilities and transit areas. A September report by the publicly funded Future of Swiss Travelers Foundation concluded authorities created only one additional permanent camping ground between the years 2010 and 2015. The foundation's director criticized the country's French-speaking region for applying "a vindictive law" against travelers' camping sites and residential caravans since 2014. During the year the Federal Office of Culture made more resources available to expedite the establishment of additional camping facilities and to raise greater social awareness about the needs of travelers.

The Swiss Roma Foundation estimated as many as 100,000 Roma resided in the country.

In July the Young Social Democrats of the canton of Bern and the Society for Threatened Peoples brought charges against a municipal councilor of the SVP for publicly stating "If you can't recognize Gypsies by plain sight, you will eventually [recognize them] with your nose." In September the Society for Threatened Peoples along with several Romani organizations pressed charges against a city hall member of the Green Liberal Party in Biel for publicly stating that all Roma lie, steal, and vandalize.

Acts of Violence, Discrimination, and Other Abuses Based on Sexual Orientation and Gender Identity

The law does not specifically ban discrimination based on sexual orientation or specifically address lesbian, gay, bisexual, transgender, and intersex (LGBTI) problems.

There were occasional reports of societal violence or discrimination based on opposition to LGBTI orientation. As of September a central office for collecting data and publishing statistics on verbal and/or physical attacks against LGBTI individuals established by LGBTI activists recorded six cases. The LGBTI umbrella NGO Pink Cross attributed the low number of cases to a lack of publicity surrounding the new office. In May a study on discrimination protection by the SCHR found that LGBTI persons experienced discrimination in the labor and housing market, while also noting problems of unequal access to general services and the judicial system.

The NGO Pink Cop (gay and lesbian police officers) noted authorities did not specifically prosecute hate crimes.

The NGO Transgender Network Switzerland criticized the requirement that changes of name and gender in official records require proof of prior diagnosis of a psychological disorder and medical procedures related to gender reassignment. The NGO also noted inadequate documenting of discrimination and hate crimes against transgender individuals and the absence of a national strategy for combating all forms of transphobia. According to the NGO, foreign and/or minor transgender individuals were at greater risk of discrimination.

In May the cantonal court of Graubuenden dismissed charges filed by Pink Cross and the Lesbian Organization of Switzerland against the bishop of Chur for inciting violence against LGBTI persons in a speech in Germany in 2015 during which he recited the passage of the Bible: "And if a man lie with mankind, as with womankind, both of them have committed abomination: they shall surely be put to death; their blood shall be upon them." Graubuenden's state prosecutor dismissed the same charges against the bishop at the end of 2015. According to Pink Cross, the organizations received many hateful telephone calls and letters from supporters of the bishop following the filing of charges.

In September the Federal Office for Gender Equality financed the online publication of support brochures about how to deal with disclosing one's gender identity in the work place. The brochures were part of a project launched by the Federal Office for Gender Equality in 2014 about problems affecting transgender persons in the workplace. The overall project was led by the Transgender Network and continued as of October.

In July parliament approved a law granting LGBTI individuals the right to adopt their partners' children. The law does not however grant LGBTI couples the right jointly to adopt children who are not biologically related. The law had not entered into force by November.

HIV and AIDS Social Stigma

There were occasional reports of discrimination against persons with HIV/AIDS. In 2015 the Swiss AIDS Federation registered 116 cases of discrimination against individuals suffering from HIV. Some 14 of the complaints concerned employment discrimination or other discrimination in the workplace (see section 7.d.). To combat harassment and unfair behavior, the Swiss AIDS Federation conducted multiple campaigns to sensitize the public to the problem.

Section 7. Worker Rights

a. Freedom of Association and the Right to Collective Bargaining

The law provides for the right for all workers, including foreigners, to form and join independent unions of their choice without previous authorization or excessive requirements. The law also provides for the right to bargain collectively and conduct legal strikes. Strikes must be linked to industrial relations. The government may curtail the right of federal public servants to strike for reasons of national security or to safeguard foreign policy interests. Laws prohibited public servants in some cantons and many municipalities from striking. No specific laws prohibit antiunion discrimination or employer interference in trade union activities. The law does not require employers to reinstate an employee whom employers unjustly dismissed for union activity.

Although the government generally enforced the law, no law defines penalties for violations of the freedoms of association or collective bargaining. Penalties took the form of fines, which were sufficient to deter violations. According to union representatives, the length of administrative and judicial procedures varied from case to case. Collective bargaining agreements committed the social partners to maintain labor peace, thereby limiting the right to strike for the duration of an agreement, which generally lasted for several years.

The freedoms of association and collective bargaining were respected by the government, but employers at times unfairly dismissed trade unionists and used the legal system to limit legitimate trade union activities. Trade unions continued to report discriminatory behavior against their members. In June the University of Neuchatel published the second part of a study commissioned by the Federal Council on the protection of workers' representatives which found that the legal protections of workers participating in lawful strikes were "full of gaps and arbitrary." The study also concluded that the country's code of obligations breached the fundamental rights and freedoms guaranteed by the International Labor Organization (ILO) and European Convention on Human Rights. The first part of the study, published in 2015, found that the labor law governing the rights to terminate work contracts does not conform to international agreements.

In 2015 the International Trade Union Confederation criticized the government for the country's repressive laws on striking.

b. Prohibition of Forced or Compulsory Labor

The law prohibits all forms of forced and compulsory labor, and the government effectively enforced such laws. Penalties for forced labor violations were up to 20 years' imprisonment and were sufficiently stringent to deter violations. The government conducted several training programs for relevant authorities on labor trafficking aimed at awareness raising and reducing such exploitation. More than 60 organizations, including trade unions and migrant associations, called on the government to implement without delay the ILO convention concerning decent work for domestic workers, since the current labor law neither applies to domestic work nor adequately regulates the working hours and rest periods of domestic workers.

There were reports that forced labor occurred. In April the University of Neuchatel released a study commissioned by the federal police that concluded forced labor occurred mainly in domestic work as well as the tourism, hospitality, construction, and agriculture industries. Women were predominantly exploited for domestic labor, while men were mostly forced to work in construction. The majority of female victims hailed from Africa and South America, while male victims predominantly came from Eastern Europe and the Balkans.

Also see the Department of State's *Trafficking in Persons Report* at www.state.gov/j/tip/rls/tiprpt/.

c. Prohibition of Child Labor and Minimum Age for Employment

The minimum age for full-time employment is 15. Children ages 13 or 14 may engage in light work for no more than nine hours per week during the school year and 15 hours at other times. Employment of youths between the ages of 15 and 18 is also restricted. Children may not work on Sundays, under hazardous conditions, or at night. The 2014 report of the ILO's Committee of Experts on the Application of Conventions and Recommendations noted that the penal code prohibits the production of pornography involving children, but the relevant provisions only cover persons less than 16 years of age.

The government effectively enforced laws and policies to protect children from exploitation in the workplace. The Federal Department of Economic Affairs, Education, and Research monitored the implementation of child labor laws and policies, and cantonal labor inspectors effectively inspected companies to determine whether there were violations of child labor laws. Cantonal inspectors strictly enforced these provisions. Violation of child labor laws is punishable by six months' imprisonment, which was sufficient to deter violations.

There were isolated reports of trafficking of children to beg and commit theft and financial frauds.

Also see Department of State's *Trafficking in Persons Report* at www.state.gov/j/tip/rls/tiprpt/.

d. Discrimination with Respect to Employment and Occupation

The equality law prohibits discrimination with respect to employment on the basis of sex. No labor law explicitly prohibits discrimination with respect to employment on the grounds of sex, race, color, religion, sexual orientation, language, political opinion, HIV-positive status or other communicable diseases, gender identity, age, or national and social origin.

Violations of the law may result in the award of compensation to a prospective or dismissed employee equal to a maximum of three months' salary in the public sector and six months' salary in the private industry. The government did not effectively enforce this provision. Penalties were not sufficient to deter violations. The ILO observed that the country lacked easily accessible mechanisms for workers to seek remedy or compensation for discrimination in employment and vocational training.

Discrimination in employment and occupation occurred with respect to national, racial, and ethnic minorities, as well as on the basis of sex, sexual orientation, gender identity, disability, HIV-positive status, and age.

Discrimination against women in the workplace is illegal, but a disproportionate share of women held jobs with lower levels of responsibility. Employers promoted women less frequently than they did men, and women were less likely to own or manage businesses. Women were heavily underrepresented in top-level management positions, particularly in private industry. The law entitles women and men to equal pay for equal work, but this was not effectively enforced. In 2014 the median monthly income for women in the public sector was 7,202 Swiss francs ($7,008), while men earned 8,208 Swiss francs ($7,987). The median monthly income for women in the private sector was 5,548 Swiss francs ($5,399), while men earned 6,536 Swiss francs ($6,360). The difference in pay between men and women was 14 percent for nonexecutive positions, while the difference for executive positions was 28 percent. Women received salaries that were on average 17 percent less than those of men in the public sector, while the average difference for the private sector was 21 percent. The pay for female university graduates was as much as 29 percent less than that of male peers in the private sector.

The Federal Office for Gender Equality financed projects that promoted equal pay and equal career opportunities in the amount of 4.4 million Swiss francs ($4.3 million). The projects were geared towards assisting businesses and counseling offices in eliminating sex-based discrimination. In September the Federal Council,

10 cantons, and 15 municipalities signed an agreement obligating the public sector and private businesses receiving government subsidies to implement equal pay for men and women.

According to Procap, one of the country's largest organizations for persons with disabilities, problems remained in integrating individuals with disabilities into the labor market, and many persons with disabilities lacked adequate support from social insurances after taking a job, which made sustained employment difficult.

In May a study on discrimination protection by the SCHR found that LGBTI persons experienced workplace discrimination, predominantly in the private sector.

In 2014 a report by the Organization for Economic Cooperation and Development (OECD) found the country's long-term unemployment rate for persons over the age of 55 was 58.6 percent in 2012, 11.4 percent above the OECD average. The OECD suggested the exclusion of age from the country's antidiscrimination law was a potential reason behind the high long-term unemployment rate of senior citizens.

In 2014 ECRI expressed concern that ethnic minorities, such as Muslims, people of color, refugees, and the Yenish and other Romani groups, experienced considerable discrimination in the labor market. According to ECRI the unemployment rate among noncitizens was 6.6 percent, compared with 2.3 percent among citizens. The report emphasized that young migrants from countries outside the EU suffered substantial discrimination, even when they had successfully completed their education in the country.

There were occasional reports of labor discrimination against persons with HIV/AIDS. In 2015 the Swiss AIDS Federation registered 116 cases of discrimination against individuals suffering from HIV. An estimated 14 of those complaints concerned employment discrimination or other discrimination in the workplace. Examples of workplace discrimination included isolated reports of workplace bullying, refusals to arrange job interviews and placements, and breaches of confidentiality about an employee's HIV-positive status.

Migrant workers in low-wage jobs were more likely than other workers to face exploitative labor practices and poor working conditions. This was especially true in the construction, hospitality, tourism, domestic work, health-care, and agricultural sectors.

e. Acceptable Conditions of Work

There was no national minimum wage. Work contracts covering approximately 40 percent of citizen wage earners included minimum wage provisions, although average wages for workers and employees covered by these contracts, particularly in the clothing, hospitality, and retail industries, remained relatively low. A majority of voluntary collective bargaining agreements, reached on a sector-by-sector basis, contained minimum compensation clauses. Numbers varied slightly from canton to canton to reflect differences in the cost of living but remained the same overall during the year. The poverty income level for a single person was 2,219 Swiss francs ($2,162) per month and 4,031 Swiss francs ($3,928) per month for a household comprising two adults and two children.

The law sets a maximum 45-hour workweek for blue- and white-collar workers in industry, services, and retail trades and a 50-hour workweek for all other workers. The rules exclude certain professions, such as taxi drivers and medical doctors. The law prescribes a rest period of 35 consecutive hours, plus an additional half-day per week. Premium pay for overtime must be at least 25 percent; overtime is generally restricted to two hours per day. The law limits annual overtime to 170 hours for those working 45 hours a week and 140 hours for those working 50 hours a week.

On January 1, a new regulation entered into force that eased the registration of working hours for employees who earn more than 120,000 Swiss francs ($116,771) per year. The government approved the new regulation after trade unions and employers reached an accord in 2015.

Employers must grant workers at least four weeks of paid vacation per year and at least five weeks to workers under the age of 20 unless the worker performs work for a third party to the detriment of the employer's legitimate interests. Workers are also entitled to one day off per week. In exceptional circumstances an employer may grant a worker two half days free instead of a full day, if required by specific work conditions and the worker consents to it.

To protect worker health and safety, the law contains extensive provisions that are current and appropriate for the main industries. Workers can remove themselves from situations that endangered health or safety without jeopardy to their employment.

The Federal Department of Economic Affairs, Education, and Research and cantonal labor inspectorates effectively enforced laws relating to hours of work and occupational safety and health across all sectors including the informal economy. In 2015 the ministry increased its labor inspections by 10 percent, covering 45,000 businesses and 175,000 individuals. The ministry also oversees collective bargaining agreements. There were approximately 100 labor inspectors, which was sufficient to enforce compliance. Each of the 26 cantons maintained a labor inspectorate office with approximately six to eight employees.

Observers did not consider penalties for labor infractions sufficient to deter violations. The courts determined fines according to the personal and economic situation of the perpetrator at the time of sentencing. In September parliament approved stricter penalties for violating minimum wage and working conditions by raising maximum monetary fines from 5,000 Swiss francs ($4,865) to 30,000 Swiss francs ($29,192).

Migrant workers in low-wage jobs, especially in the construction, hospitality, tourism, domestic, agricultural, and health care sectors, were more likely to experience exploitative labor practices. During the year several local NGOs and international organizations, including the International Organization for Migration, expressed concern authorities were not adequately addressing labor exploitation prevalent in the construction, hospitality, health-care, and domestic-labor sectors. In March the Federal Council established a national action plan for better combating labor law breaches and labor exploitation.

Immigrants may work and have the same rights as other workers. There are no special provisions or requirements for noncitizen workers, apart from having legal immigration status and a valid work permit. The government did not allow individuals without legal status or work permits to work. Individuals who obtained legal status could request a work permit. Asylum seekers were usually not allowed to work during the first three to six months after they had applied for asylum but in exceptional cases could work as self-employed as needed.

The Federal Office for Health convened a roundtable of industry, trade union, and NGO representatives that decided to develop a fund worth 100 million Swiss francs ($97.3 million) for assisting asbestos victims who had been diagnosed with cancer dating back to 2006. The fund will be financed by voluntary industry contributions. In April the Federal Court ceased compensation proceedings for asbestos victims and referred the cases to the roundtable for deliberation following trade unions' demands for the forum in 2014.